A Beauty.Full Mind

A Beauty. Full Mind

CARLA CHATBURN

Secrets to Salon Success

CONTENTS

INTRODUCTION

There is so much about the beauty industry that I wish I'd known sooner. After twenty years of working in this business, I know that my journey could have been easier if someone had sat me down and told me what I'm about to tell you. And not just the obvious things like how to do an eyebrow wax without ripping off the whole eyebrow – yes, I really did that! – but about the challenging thoughts and feelings that I was going to experience on my journey.

The beauty industry has very high standards, but with it comes a lot of pressure that you wouldn't expect: how to feel confident 24/7 when inside you might be quite shy or having a bad day. Maybe you have dreams of becoming self-employed but feel overwhelmed at all the other skills that you'd have to learn. Perhaps you've worked in beauty for a while now, but you're burnt out. Or you're becoming a manager for the first time, but you feel awkward in this new leadership role.

I want you to know that I had all the same fears. As a profession, working in beauty is absolutely incredible. It's fast-paced, innovative, creative and you'll never get bored. But I wasn't ready for what the 12-hour shifts and weekend work would really be like.

I got into beauty because I was drawn to the sheer bling of it. Like a magpie, I was just in awe of the sparkle, the shimmer and the glamour. But, at the same time, I had to learn the hard way how to deal with the 'blonde bimbo' comments, and push through the soul-crushing moments of self-doubt and anxiety. No one told me how awkward I would feel at business events, or how intimidating I would find other entrepreneurial and successful women. There were so many times during my journey when I wished I had felt more empowered and confident to reach out for help when I needed it.

So, this is why I am writing this book for you and why I created The Confident Beauty Therapist Programme. There will be times in your beauty career when you will feel like I did, so I want to empower you and help you to feel more confident when those thoughts and feelings come up. No matter where your strengths and weaknesses lie, I want to help you turn them into your superpowers, so you can break out of your comfort zone and feel confident in whatever goal you set for yourself. Trust me when I say that if you remain curious, open-minded and humble, you will become a confident beauty therapist. I mean, just look at you now! Just being here, reading this book, and being open to learning proves that you have what it takes.

In the following chapters, you'll read my story of twenty years of working in beauty. I now run and own three award-winning salons, I have 25 professional industry awards to my name, and I have trained and supported over 100 apprentices and staff in their beauty careers. But getting here wasn't easy.

You will hear about what it was like to open my first salon at the age of 21 and all the silly mistakes that I made. I'll tell you what it's like to deal with imposter syndrome, and how I managed my limiting beliefs around money. I'll tell you why I decided to go back to school to get a teaching degree, while at the same time still running my business. I also want to share with you the story of what happened when I got diagnosed with dyslexia, why I have a business coach, and what happened when COVID hit the beauty industry.

We all have different journeys to take in this world, and mine is just one of many. But we do all have the same worries and questions, and I want to normalise them for you, and remind you that you aren't alone. You can be anything you want to be if you work really, really hard, but you have to be dedicated and driven. You have to be accountable, humble and be willing to learn. If that sounds like you, then you will find value in this book.

So, without any more delay, let's get started with Chapter 1, and the story of where it all started.

THE
CONFIDENT *Beauty* THERAPIST
PROGRAMME

Passion for Perfection creates excellence. Always take pride in your work. You are the artist in your beauty journey.

THE
CONFIDENT *Beauty* THERAPIST
PROGRAMME

Take the time and try the treatments so you know how it feels. Its a great learning experience for you and your clients.

THE
CONFIDENT
THERAPIST
PROGRAMME

**Only I can
change my life,
No one can
do it for me**

Carol burnett

*Create your own opportunities, don't wait for the right time. Are you
taking personal accountability?*

First salon, age 21, Pure Perfection est 2005, Accrington, Hyndburn, Lancashire. Recognition to Adele.

Professional beauty 2021 interview shoot for Employer of the Year award. Photo credits to Sam Fenton.

1. THE TRUTH ABOUT BEAUTY

D o you want to know a secret? It's something that I used to be ashamed of, but I think you should know: I'm not an academic person. From an early age, I knew that my school studies were not going to be a strength of mine. Let's just say that I was very much away with the fairies. I was a real people-pleaser, and because I was quite a shy person and a bit of an introvert, I was very easily influenced – and sometimes misled – by people who appeared more confident or self-assured than me. That doesn't sound like someone who would become an award-winning businesswoman, does it? But, I want you to know that it doesn't matter who you are or what your background is, you have the skills that will make you a brilliant beauty therapist. You just have to find them. For me, not being a traditionally academic person meant that I just had to use the other skills that I had.

When I was younger, I knew pretty quickly that nobody was coming to save me. No one was going to give me the confidence that I needed, or make me better at school. The only way that I was going to get anywhere in life was to do it myself. My dad left home when I was about three or four years old, leaving my mum to raise me and my sister, Adele, on her own. I had to watch my mum struggle financially and emotionally, but as hard as it was, she instilled in me a really strong work ethic. She taught me that you have to show up, no matter what. She taught me not to rely on anyone else, because only you are responsible for your own career path. There wasn't going to be a knight in shining armour, or a rich aunt who was going to come and save the day.

So, when I discovered the beauty industry, it was like, 'Yes! I've found it!' This was going to be my ticket to success. And maybe you feel like this too. I might not have been good at academics, but I was a people-pleaser. Making people feel good about themselves was a drive I had inside me, and I'd just discovered the job where I could do that all day, every day. It gave me the courage that I needed to explore this industry, and I knew that if I could just stay on this path, I was prepared to give it my all. I had found my passion.

When I was fourteen, I went and found myself a Saturday job. It was at a hairdressers called The Hairdressers (yes, really!), just making brews and washing hair. It was the first time that I'd experienced the culture of what working in hair and beauty would be like. Being around all these creative and talented people gave me the confidence to explore beauty on my own. I'm a naturally curious person, and I learn more by doing. So, I bought myself a little 99p pack of fake nails from a supermarket and just sat at home and played with them. And let me tell you, I made my bitten-down nails look beautiful; I felt like a million dollars. That feeling of making something look better made me feel so good inside. I knew instantly that I wanted to go into beauty.

But I had a problem: I didn't have the money for traditional training. Whenever I walked past a new salon, or saw a beauty therapist working for themselves, I would think: *How could they afford to do that?* That was the bit that intrigued me, because I had very little money. I come from quite a humble background and I had lived in several homes provided by housing associations. I remember one in particualar with no carpet on the stairs, but my mum always found a way to make it feel like home. Even so, I deeply wanted to try a different path. I liked the thought of being in a salon, actively training while earning, so I took a beauty apprenticeship. It wasn't a lot, maybe £60 a week back then, but I was like, 'I'll take it!' It was like a taste of freedom, learning whilst getting paid. But it was here, during my apprenticeship, that I learned that the beauty industry isn't always as glam as it looks.

The Other Side of Glam

People often go into the beauty industry for the wrong reasons and I'm guilty of this too. I was naive when I started. I've been educating apprentices for over twenty years and they all have the same misconception of what the beauty industry is like. If you had told me that I'd have toenails flick into my mouth or go home with bikini wax hairs stuck to my clothes, I might have thought twice about beauty. Indeed, housekeeping and cleaning toilets were not what I had planned for my beauty career.

You need to be prepared to meet some very interesting characters, and have conversations that are absolutely mad. I was once asked out on a date in the middle of a back, sack and crack wax. When it happened, I just froze. I remember thinking: *What do I say now?* I was in a professional environment in a really awkward situation; they didn't teach me this during my beauty apprenticeship! Thankfully, he quickly realised that what he did was wrong and the moment passed. But how do you prepare for situations like that? You have to be ready for anything that this business throws at you, and it's why I've added modules on courage, emotional intelligence and confidence to the CBT [The Confident Beauty Therapist) programme.

Working in the beauty industry also means that you are more likely to be judged on how *you* look: if you don't have nice nails, for example, how will your clients trust that you can do their nails too? You have to show confidence in yourself and what you can provide. After all, first impressions count and you have just three seconds to make somebody feel good about being in your presence. This is a people-first industry. It's all about relationships and building trust, so you've got to be a people person. You've got to genuinely like people and people have to be able to like you too. OK, you don't have to be everyone's best friend, but your clients have to find your personality positive and engaging if they're going to keep coming back.

I have a story about one of my team members. She was absolutely brilliant, but, to be fair, she was in the wrong industry. When she failed her probationary period with me, she admitted, 'I can't do a poker face like you do.' And I love that she called me out on this. At first, I was confused. 'I don't have a poker face,' I said. What did she mean by that? But then, I realised she was right. I do have a poker face. We all do. You do too. It's part of this industry. If you're not able to smile at your clients and make them feel welcome, even when you're tired or in a bad mood, this industry is not for you.

This industry is about making your clients feel their best, and that means putting them first. Treat your clients as the diamonds they are, and I guarantee you that you'll be rewarded in ways you never imagined. And if you're reading this and starting to worry: *What if I'm not good with people? What if I can't do it?* I want you to know that you can. Because anything can be learned. Any skill can be improved.

Knowledge is Power

Whenever I saw a salon owner, I was just in awe of their achievements. I was also curious: *How did they do that?* I would wonder. *Where did they get the confidence from?* I knew that I had to find a different way to build success, so I used the resources that were available to me. Knowledge is definitely power, so, when I was starting out, Google was my best friend. After all, it was free. If there was something that I didn't know, and I didn't feel comfortable asking someone, I would ask Google.

I remember once going to a networking event and someone had used the word 'strategy.' I had never heard that word before, and I thought, 'Oh, I'm out of my comfort zone now. I haven't a clue what that means.' So I googled it, and found out that it was just a fancy word for 'plan.' When I opened my second salon, someone said to me, 'You're really getting into this entrepreneurial spirit, aren't you?' and I just smiled at them, but I was thinking, *What on earth does 'entrepreneurial' mean?* So I asked Google. Here I was, being an entrepreneur, and I didn't know what 'entrepreneurial' meant.

Don't assume that everyone you meet has all the answers. In my opinion, there's no silly question that you can ask, and honestly I've asked some of the stupidest questions ever. But I used that to my advantage, and that curiosity helped me to build a career. For me, curiosity is a massive drive. You don't know what you don't know, but if you're passionate about what you love and which direction you're going in, and your curiosity is insane – use it. If you don't know or understand something, it's not a failure, just use it as an opportunity to ask a question that will move you forward in your career.

It's All About to Change

I know you are going to have so many questions on the journey ahead, and I don't want you to struggle like I did. Going into business blind was the most exhausting process that I've ever been through. This is because I had to learn everything three times: going backward and forward, and failing twice before I got it right. I reached out to friends to help me with marketing or law and I asked so many questions. I bet they got so annoyed at me, but I needed to know. I couldn't afford to hire people to do it for me. If you have friends who can help you, then reach out and get advice from them that relates to their skill set. There is so much more to the beauty industry than making your clients look good. You have to feel as beautiful and confident on the inside as you do on the outside, and that's why this book is going to help you.

Since working in this industry, my idea of what I thought confidence was has changed. I thought it was the loud flamboyant characters that you see in salons, but, in reality, it's about knowing who you are and being confident and comfortable with that. It's knowing your strengths and weaknesses, and being OK with that. I didn't realise it at the time, but I think I saw beauty as my chance to be someone else. It was such a creative industry that I was able to express myself in a different way, and become a new person. I wanted to feel accepted and part of the team, so I always adapted myself to suit the environment, and I became a chameleon. But it was only because I was frightened to death of not fitting in. Whenever I stepped out of my comfort zone, it really was a case of faking it until you make it, on every level of my journey.

But I want you to know that I had to grow and change in order to get where I am today. There was a lot of self-discovery and hard work involved in understanding who I was, so that I could feel confident in my work. So, I ask you to have an open mind. We only ever see the glitz and glamour in this industry, but in reality it's so much more. It's about the people – what their needs are and how you treat them. The creativity that you find in this industry is wonderful and it is a big driver for many people going into it, but there's also a lot to do with business – about profit and loss, about mindset and resilience. It's about investing in personal growth, continued learning and professional development – a lot of the things that I bet you never thought you'd have to think about. Don't think that once you're working and you've finished your training, it ends there. Whatever path you take in beauty, if you want to be successful then my first biggest lesson for you is that you should never stop learning.

Core Beauty Tips

1. Be curious. Knowledge is power, so go and ask the silly questions and don't be afraid of what people might think or say. If you can learn from someone who's doing well, reach out to them. If you came to me and asked me for help, I would always want to help you, and so should the people you reach out to.

2. Don't judge a book by its cover. If you see someone who is confident and assured, don't assume that they might not be struggling too. Don't assume that just because someone owns a salon, or has a skill you don't, it means they know it all. Remember, just because it looks perfect on the outside, it doesn't mean it's perfect on the inside.

3. Keep your circle small. There's a belief that we have to have a ton of friends and a huge network in this industry, but if that's too much for you, keeping your circle small can be just as helpful. Connect with people who you can trust, who have actually walked the walk and who can give facts and figures about the journey ahead.

4. Be open. This business has so many paths open to you; it's just about finding the right route for you. You don't have to stick to the first beauty skill that you go into; try a few out and see what you like. But be realistic and don't expect results straight away. It will take time to find your place, and that's perfectly normal. You may find out that your strengths aren't client-facing but that they lie somewhere else, like in management or education.

5. Don't compare yourself to anyone in the beauty industry or to their business. The models will be different. The client base will be different. Your values and thinking will be different. Your understanding of success will be different. You can't compare yourself to anyone. And, if you do, you'll have a lifelong career of 'I'm not good enough.' So, don't waste your time comparing!

It's never just a nail service. It's art, skill, creativity and making your clients feel the best version of themselves.

It's the little details that count. They say more you than you think.

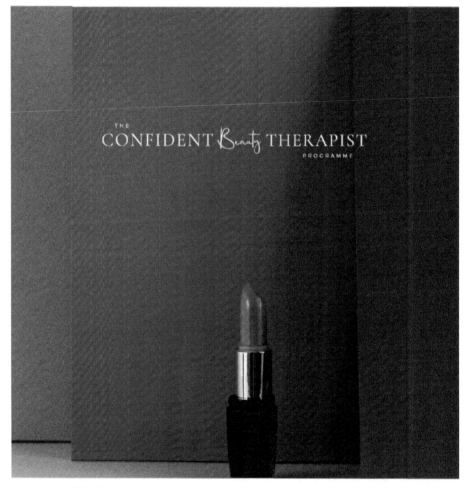

Too glam to give a damn, find your authentic self and work on your awareness in you and others.

We can learn a lot from trees: they're always grounded but never stop reaching heavenward.

Everett Mamor

Keep your feet firmly on the ground but reach for the stars. It's the journey that bring wealth in all areas of life.

2. MINDING THE OPINIONS OF OTHERS

Nobody knows this, but when I opened my first salon, I would come home and cry. *A lot.* I was very much a private person so I never showed anyone what I was going through. I made it all about everybody else. However, deep down, I was absolutely dying, worrying that I wasn't good enough to run a salon. I kept asking myself: 'How do I even do this? I've not got a business degree. What am I doing?'

From a very early age, I had a really strong work ethic and was super independent. My aunt had once said to me, 'Follow your dreams. You only live once.' She had written those heartfelt words to me from her hospital bed. She was sick with cancer at the time; she was only 36 years old. A few days after giving me that advice, she died. At the time, I don't think I could really process it. She was a career-driven woman. She had a daughter. A husband. I was in awe of her and inspired by her. And it didn't seem fair that that could happen.

So, when I saw a salon available for rent on Warner street, in Accrington, I felt like I had sparks of fire in my belly. Sheer passion. 'I need to do it. If I don't do it now, I could die tomorrow,' I thought. I could work; I had the skills. *What's the worst thing that could happen?* That same day, I rang my stepdad and I said, 'I've just seen a shop and I need it. Please just come and have a look at it with me.' It was a two-storey stone terraced building with plain cream walls and concrete floors. It was just a bare, blank canvas. Nothing at all inside. It was really cheeky but my stepdad managed to blag one months' free rent from the landlord. I was so excited. I was like, 'This is amazing!' But my stepdad warned me. He said, 'Right. Here's six and a half grand for the deposit. You've got three months to make it work.' My mum was not currently working. My real dad was a drug addict. I had no choice but to make this work. Failure was not an option. I was ready. Thanks to the love and support of my family I finally had the keys to my first salon, and it felt amazing. My dream could not have started if it weren't for them, and this made me even more determined to succeed. There I was, finally a salon owner. I was only 21 years old… and I had no idea what I was getting myself into. Failure was not an option. I was ready. I became a salon owner. I was only 21 years old and I had no idea what I was getting myself into.

Managing Imposter Syndrome

Never feeling good enough has been one of my main driving forces. I was bullied pretty much throughout my entire school years, and I used to be frightened to death of the words that people would say. So, I was always striving for perfection, in everything I did. On the first day of opening my salon, I ended up working for 12 hours and I only had two customers. The door said that I was open from 9 a.m. till 9 p.m., so I had to do it. But there was still a little voice in my head saying, 'You're not enough, Carla. You can do better.' So, I gritted my teeth and was like, 'That's OK. Two people. Let's keep going.' The next day followed and then the next, and within three months I was booked up to the point that I needed help.

It sounds so easy when I put it like that – that all you have to do is work hard and you'll magically get there. However, I want you to know that there were lots of ups and downs on my journey. I would get passive aggressive comments like, 'Oh, she just does nails.' People would dismiss me by saying, 'What a beauty therapist bimbo.' I heard all these comments, and allowed a lot of negative messages into my head. On top of that, I had my own negative thoughts that came from inside me too, from a place of fear and low self-esteem.

At the same time, I wanted to prove everyone wrong. I wanted to prove myself wrong. I knew that I was good enough but I had a real fear of failure, so when someone gave me negative feedback, I had no option but to make it better. I would ask myself: *Why did they say that?* And start looking for the answer. *Did I really do something wrong? Was the service really that bad?* It didn't occur to me to let it stop me, I saw it as a sign that I had to do better. I was striving for perfection. Through my entire career, I've taken every negative comment that someone gave me and I've run with it. Don't get me wrong, it still hurt. I would still cry, but I used it to push me forward.

I once got a negative review that said that my treatment beds were not warm enough. I could have sat at home and been sad, or I could go out and get better treatment couches and put bed warmers on. So, I did that. It was an experience that I had to go through and I want you to know that it didn't come easily. Every comment hurt. Every bad word made me feel awful. But, by using the negative feedback to your advantage, you can make things better – you can make your business better. I really care about people's opinions and you might see it as a weakness. But, turn it over and see it as a strength. I use it to create excellence and it's why I have award-winning salons.

Don't let negative comments stop you from trying, and from making those mistakes. It's part of the journey. And sometimes making those mistakes can give you some funny stories. I once needed to practise doing eyebrows but I didn't feel comfortable working on a paying client. So, I reached out to a friend for help. She said, 'Yeah, OK, it's free.' Well . . . I only went and waxed one of her eyebrows completely off her face! It wasn't funny at the time; in fact, I think we both cried. 'I'm never waxing eyebrows ever again,' I said in horror. She had to go home with ONE eyebrow, didn't she?

I've done spray tans for people and forgotten to do their inner thighs because I was just chatting away. It's probably not the best service I could have given them, but when you're learning and growing, these things are going to happen. It's normal. I've caught a couple of cuticles on client's fingernails and toenails; there is a little bit of blood present and it looks bad, but you manage the process and make sure that the wound is cleaned and covered up. There's a process for everything, and part of that process is just not to panic.

Honesty is the best policy. If you've messed up – if someone criticises you or your business – hold your hand up and apologise. Clients will have much more respect for you if you do. If you are having a bad day, or if the product didn't work as well as it should or a customer just didn't feel like they were valued, it's important that you reach out to clients and ask for the feedback. It's not the end of the world and you find a way to get better.

Obviously I don't want to encourage you to think it's acceptable to go around making mistakes all the time, but things do happen. We're not robots; we aren't going to be perfect every day, no matter how hard you try. So don't be too hard on yourself. Find a way to make sure that you never make that mistake again. And even if you do make the mistake again, it's not the end of the world. If I'd quit when I'd got things wrong, I wouldn't be where I am now, with three amazing salons and a range of business awards with a professional dedicated team.

Your Money Mindset

When people first start running their businesses, whether self-employed or in a salon, they're often not aware of their money mindset. And I do think it's an important thing to consider. When I opened that first salon, never in my life had I seen that amount of money. It wasn't a lot but it was to me at that time. I was a naive little girl and I didn't realise that the money you see and the money you don't see are two very different things. I was in awe of what I thought financial wealth really was. I thought it was the big house and the fancy cars, the Louis Vuittons. But I was a kid, with no financial education and no financial backup – should anything go wrong. I ended up maxing out my mum's credit cards, and spent thirteen and a half thousand pounds before I'd even opened the salon. I took the approach of, 'Yeah, I can do this. Let's not think about the consequences.' I knew it was my priority to pay my debts back first. But, in order for a business to grow, I had to change the way that I thought about money.

Lots of people have limiting beliefs about money, and I did too. I believed that if you've got lots of money, you're a horrible person. You're selfish if you want to have lots of money and all of that. But I want you to know that wanting and having money does not make you a bad person. *It's what you do with the money that determines who you are.*

I bought myself all these amazing things, and, rightly so, I've put in the time and effort to create that wealth. I've worked for it, but I always gave back to others along the way. If someone doesn't have the desire to work hard, they can't expect to have the money they want. It creates resentment, and I think that's where they start judging people who have financial success and where we get these negative messages around money. People don't talk enough about money, especially women, so let's change that and open the conversation. I came from a background where money was tight, so I'm no longer ashamed to say that getting more money became one of my main drivers.

For the first four years of running my business, I lived at home. And I knew I couldn't leave home until I had a sustainable income. It was a turning point in my understanding and I started thinking, 'OK, I need to be paid *this* in order to get to *that* point, and my staff need to be paid before I get paid, so I need to make X amount of money. But then the companies that provide my products need to get paid. And I've got rent on the salon. So, really *this* is how much money I need to be paid.' It sounds really simple but you'd be surprised by how people just don't think carefully about money like that. It's that thought process that led me to come up with the policies and procedures that were needed to help grow my company. It made me realise that I needed to learn more about money: about bookkeeping, and profit and loss accounts. I began to understand why I'd see multimillion pound companies generate all this money, but then have nothing left in the pot. And if you have nothing left in the pot, what's the point? Working on my mindset around money was an eye-opening experience and I recommend that you also work on yours.

When you understand how money works, you can invest in others and help people to grow – and that's when you start using money for good. It can be a great source of happiness, and what's wrong with that? At this point in my life, I understand my money mindset, and while I actually earn *less* now, I'm much more rich in how much free time I have. I pay people to do the work that I don't have time to do, because I want to spend more time with my family. It is through understanding money – and my relationship and mindset around it – that I have been able to do that.

How to approach your money will depend on what's important to you. Do you want more time, or do you want more money? Or do you want more self-development? Having a good money mindset is not about how you make money, it's how you use money to achieve your goals. It's what you do with it on your journey, how you invest it, and how you use it. To me, money is not success. It's just a byproduct. To some people, driving a nice car or living in a big house is not success, it's spending their money on holidays and only working part time so that they can spend more time with people they love. It's up to you to decide what money is going to do for you.

If you're unsure of how to start when it comes to money, here are a few basic rules:

Give it Back

If you do get the wealth, give it back. Every penny that I earned during my first six years of business, I invested back into the company rather than myself. I invested in people, and in education and skills. I might not have paid myself a wage for those first years, but I was always investing in my education. Invest in your personal growth, too, because even if you make lots of money, it will not fix your personal problems; it will just bring more. Trust me on that one.

Learn About Money

I always thought success was how big your turnover was. So, in my naivety, I was striving for my turnovers to be bigger and bigger and bigger. I genuinely thought that everything that went into the till was mine. I was like, 'God, businesses is so easy!' But as my turnover got bigger, my profit margins became lower and lower and lower. On the outside, I looked like I was making more money, but, actually, my net profit margins became so much smaller. I didn't understand where the money was going. It was tough. Honestly, I never had a clue about what all that meant and I had to learn while I was doing it. Like I said, I'm not an academic person so I had to really focus hard, but investing in my education around money has helped me to grow my business. And it will help you too.

Pay Back Your Debt

The money that I had used to open my salon wasn't mine – it was a loan. I knew how hard money was to come by, and it was important to me to pay every penny back. You will always be living in the past with your debts so make it your number one priority to pay it back, then you can focus on your future profits and what you can do with them to grow professionally and personally.

Put Your Business First

Being the last person in the business to get paid made me learn different ways to manage money, and it made me work even harder to drive the company forward. If I wanted to pay myself, I had to get my company in a good place. You could say it was quite a naive approach to business. However, by making one of my key drivers ensuring that everyone else was cared for, I was pushed in the right direction. I had to make sure that all my product providers were paid and up to date, and I had to make sure that the team were paid before me. After all, without a team, you haven't got a business. I just didn't realise how it all worked; I didn't even know what the profit margins were in my services. I just delivered a service and hoped for the best; it's kind of like doing business backwards.

It's all 'Figure-Out-Able'

Slowly, over time, I realised, *Wow, I can do this. I can do anything I put my mind to.* But I wish I'd known I didn't have to do it alone. I didn't have to come home and cry alone. I didn't have to put on a brave face when people said horrible things. I should have asked for help when I was struggling. But, I didn't know you could. I didn't know what I didn't know. I didn't have a circle of friends who understood business, or a community that could give me the answers. I didn't have a business coach, and I didn't have anyone I could talk to. At that point, Google was my closest friend in business.

If you don't know something, if you feel out of your depth, don't be afraid to learn. It will be your biggest driver of success. And remember that those emotions you're going to feel when you start are normal. The fear, the worry and the doubt. It's normal and it's OK to feel like that. You don't need to take things personally, but if your client has a criticism, it needs to be heard. That's what they value. It's a value that you can adapt to and change with, or it's a value you can ignore. It's up to you.

Core Beauty Tips

1. It's OK to make mistakes. It's like passing the first driving test. You're going to hit bumps along the road; you're going to have a couple of crashes. But it's about picking yourself back up and not being hard on yourself. We all make mistakes.

2. When you try something, don't quit. Give it three goes, at least. And that is when the magic starts happening. You have to action your new skills and you have to believe. Whether it's academic, or a physical skill, you have to do something with what you've learned.

3. Keep asking for feedback. It keeps you on your toes. If you stop trying to learn and improve, your standards will slip and that's not good for you or your business.

4. Keep the end goal in sight. It will be tough, especially when people judge you. But I had to remind myself constantly of the end goal; 'It's going to be worth it', I would think. It's kind of like your internal vision board. Just keep that vision, stay focused, and remember why you're doing it.

5. Enjoy the journey. If you don't enjoy what you're doing, it will be so hard for you and all those negative messages will get to you. You've got to enjoy what you're doing and know it's worth it.

THE
CONFIDENT *Beauty* THERAPIST
PROGRAMME

11.2 / ―

WE
CARE

Care about your work and you will find success in every part of your journey.

Most smiles are started by another smile.

Anon

Wear your smile as your logo, it's free and means more to others than you will ever know.

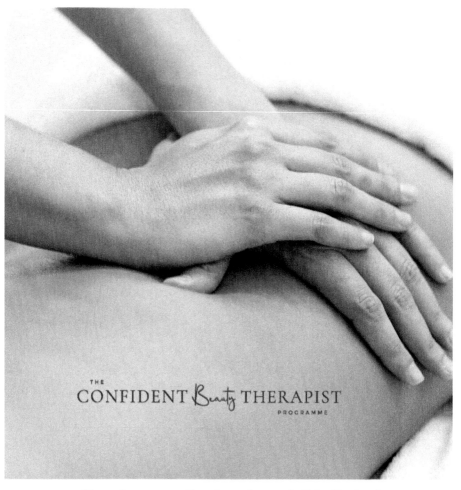

It's more than a massage, it's me time, and so many health benefits externally and internal. Self care is not selfish.

em·pow·er

/əmˈpou(ə)r/ verb

make (someone) stronger and more confident, especially in controlling their life and claiming their rights.

@CONFIDENTBEAUTY

Behind every successful woman is a tribe of other successful women who have her back.

Pure Perfection, est 2013 Clitheroe, Ribble Valley, Lancashire.
Recognition to Tara.

3. CHANGING MY MIND

The first time that I went to a lecture at the University of Central Lancashire, I was absolutely pooping myself. I had just enrolled in my teaching degree course but I wasn't prepared for how anxious I'd feel on that first day. Even though I put on my confident face, deep down I was terrified. My anxiety was sky-high. I was sweating. I was the only beauty therapist in a lecture room full of lawyers, nurses, teachers and professionals. I felt like I was out of my depth. What was I doing here?

Back to School

Let's rewind. Only two months before, I had opened up my own salon in Accrington, Lancashire. However, I had quickly realised that I'd been naive to think that you can run a business on your own. You've got to ask for help. I very quickly got to the point where I needed to hire a qualified therapist, but I couldn't afford one, so my only option was to hire an apprentice and run an apprenticeship programme. But I didn't want to do just any programme; I wanted it to be the best. If I was going to train people in beauty and have them work in my salon, they had to have a better education and support system than I'd ever had.

When I'd been an apprentice, there was a lot that got missed. And you might feel the same if you've been one too.

During my apprenticeship, no one ever taught me how to run my own salon or anything about the roles and responsibilities of leading a team. I was never taught how to manage my money mindset, or confidence, or to have courage when things went wrong. Some of the programmes were just opportunities for cheap labour disguised as apprenticeships. I wanted my apprentices to feel part of the business. You have to feel like you have opportunities and a path for growth, don't you? At the end of the day, I knew I couldn't grow my business without them, so I had to give them everything they needed to be the best they could be.

But how do I do all of that? Where do you start? How do I teach someone properly, if I've never taught before? To give my learners the best possible outcome, I had to learn how to teach and so I put myself on that course. However, as I sat in that lecture room, I felt out of place. I had never felt good enough to be in those rooms, and even though I was starting that degree, I felt like I was unworthy – surely I didn't deserve to be in this environment with all these intelligent people. I was just a beauty therapist. I felt like I didn't have anything to add to the conversation. But, I was a great listener and observer, and so I did what I did best. You could call it my survival technique to get me through that learning experience. Anything that I didn't understand I would note down and then run to ask Google when I got home.

Even though I was quite naive, I am a curious person. I wanted my journey to be so different to what I had as a child, so I got on a hamster wheel of sheer education and knowledge. I may have felt like I didn't belong in that room, but I was here now, and I was going to learn as much as I could. When I went into the beauty industry I was seen as a bimbo that just files nails, and I lived up to that. If that's how I was perceived, why fight against it? But I think too many women feel like that, and that kind of thinking limits your future potential, your earning power and your success. I didn't know it at the time, but I had that fire in me to reach for more. Getting this degree was something that I had to achieve, and I'm so glad that I did because it changed my future.

Investing in Your People

There are so many different routes to take to get into beauty. Some people just want to be a one-man band, and I work with many people in my salon who aren't on my payroll but are self-employed. However, I knew early on that I wanted more. I wanted that nice car and the big house, so I knew I had to go bigger. If I wanted to take my business to the next level, I had to update my knowledge, take on the roles and responsibilities of an employer, and become an authority figure.

I never went into the industry to be a leader; I still struggle to see myself like that, even today. I was very much a submissive person and I just wanted everyone to be happy. However, I soon realised that to grow a successful business, you do have to learn certain qualities. And, by the way, I didn't know at the time that this is what I had to do. Everything that I was doing at this point was instinctive and unconscious. I was just following my belief about how to be a good beauty therapist. So, don't feel like you're doing anything wrong if your path isn't clear yet.

I took on an apprentice halfway through my degree, because I needed the support in the salon, but I also had to demonstrate competence at delivering what I was learning. You don't know what you don't know and it really shocked me to see how much work went into educating someone: all the legal implications, all the work, observations and documentation that you need in order to ensure that a learner gets what they need. It's a business in itself. I was exposed very quickly to different learning styles and how different personalities clash with these learning styles, and I formed a strong understanding of how important clear and honest communication was.

Within the first year of opening my salon, and because the client demand was exceptional, I ended up taking on two apprentices. However, I soon realised that I had to change the way that I thought about working with people. When you become an employer, there are three people in a beauty relationship: you, your employee and the client. We are all people-pleasers in this industry, so when it comes to asserting ourselves, or following through on policies and procedures, we struggle. We don't want to hurt someone's feelings, and that obstacle was a massive eye-opener for me. Not only will you have to manage clients' expectations, you will have to manage your team's and your own.

You have to work hard at building up that respectful relationship so that your apprentices, and your staff, feel comfortable asking the stupid questions – which I love. I love the stupid questions, because that's how I learned. I encouraged my apprentices to ask for pay rises, and to step outside their comfort zones without being fearful of the consequences.

If you ever take on an apprentice, you will soon learn that everyone has different drivers and motivators in their careers. Some people are driven by money and targets, and some people aren't. I was shocked, and it was a real mind block for me – I thought everyone was driven by money! You can lead a horse to water, but you can't make it drink, and I had to learn how to motivate my team in other ways that weren't around money. I was always asking: how could I make my apprenticeship programme better? How can we help our staff so that they don't feel X, Y and Z? I didn't want anyone to ever feel like I did –worthless or unimportant – so I was real and open and honest with them about everything. If they had a questions about sales, or the numbers or marketing, I told them. I would tell them where the money was going and they knew the reasons behind every decision I made. Doing it like this meant that I built a team of open and honest therapists who could support each other, even when I wasn't there.

I wanted to make sure that even though I was running a business, I was still accommodating their needs because you don't have a business without your team. And if you're not harming anyone, then try it. If somebody wants to develop in the business, find a way to give them opportunities. If somebody wants to earn more money, find a way to get them more responsibilities and new job roles. And if somebody only wants to work part time, find a way that would work well for them and the business. It's just about being curious and exploring different avenues.

I wanted to create a very clear path for anyone who worked with me where they could grow with me and my business, rather than leave. It was a case of having a 'train and retain' mindset. But that doesn't mean that you won't have challenges as you grow. Once, I hit a stumbling block where one of my team members – who I had spent a couple of years working with, who was also one of my first apprentices – wanted to leave to go travelling. And I found myself getting upset. Obviously, business is business, and I had to quickly learn to keep the two relationships very, very separate. I wished her well and said, 'Go, spread your wings. But if you ever come back, my door will be open.' And I meant it. A business should always accommodate its people, not the other way around. So she went abroad, but as soon she got back, she got in touch and said, 'I want to come back. Do you have any positions for me?' At that time, I couldn't give her a position because there wasn't enough client demand. But, she was worth investing in. I already trusted her. I already knew her work ethic. I knew her personality and what her main drivers were. So, I said, 'How about you open another salon for me? I'll fund it all. You just go away and make it your own. Are you up for the challenge?' Now, at that point, I had no idea how I was going to pay for it. You might think I'm mad, but I took a big risk in investing in her, and in opening the second location, but it paid off – and that became my Pure Perfection salon number two. Worst case scenario, if it didn't work, I would put myself in the Clitheroe salon, my second salon. By then, I had the confidence to build a client base and train someone else up. I also had another therapist who had been going above and beyond; her clients were flying in and she wanted growth and a financial reward. So, I felt confident leaving her in the salon with a new management role if I needed to go to the second salon. Loyalty is a big thing for me, and I knew she was worth investing in.

It is priceless to have people that you can trust and who you've built strong relationships with. And if you have someone in your business that's loyal and respectful of policies and procedures, they're like gold. Investing in people in this way means that you will have a team around you that you can trust to deliver the service that you want them to. It will give you the freedom to take risks and think about building the business. But also, it will give you the freedom to not feel so alone when building your business.

Relationships drive the beauty industry, so if you don't have a good relationship with your client, or your staff, it's very easy for them to go elsewhere. In business, the ROI (I didn't figure out that this meant 'return on investment' until ten years later) isn't always financial – it can be relationship-based. I invested in staff, and I got a return on my investment – and they got what they wanted out of the situation as well. We work in such a lovely industry that nothing can go wrong if you treat people with kindness and compassion. Be true to yourself and you will attract people that are like you.

Invest in Yourself

Changing my mindset around education and people has been one of the biggest and best lessons I've ever had. We're not robots, we've got to learn somehow, and this process of changing the way that I thought took many years and lots of mistakes. I wish I hadn't been so hard on myself when I was studying. I am my own worst critic, but at the time it was my choice to go on that course and it enabled me to have the life I have now. So, when you choose to invest your time, invest in what's important to you. I knew I had to invest in my own education because I knew I had very little knowledge in terms of what I needed to do to go forward. I knew I had to invest in people, because without them I wouldn't have a business. It was a more intuitive, more instinctive way of working, probably not something that you would expect, but it worked for me. And if it's a style that you like, and you think it will work for you, then try it. There is no right or wrong, you can only try and see what works. If things don't happen right the first time, it doesn't mean you're a failure. I had to do a lot of work on changing my limiting beliefs, changing my processes and policies, and changing the way that I communicated with people.

If I had to break down the past 20 years of my career, I have not got a clue how I have ended up in this position. However, the only thing that I can say to anybody who is striving for success, which is personal to everyone, is to take baby steps, because nothing's going to happen overnight. And it really is taking that one step at a time, building that confidence, and then exploring different options. Success is different to different people and everyone measures it differently, so it really does depend on what you want out of this career and what success means to you.

Core Beauty Tips

1. Explore non-traditional routes for education. I reached out to government support networks and found funding for half of the degree, and used all the business profits I made at that time plus a small personal loan to fund the rest. Again, this wasn't the normal path for a university programme but that was the only way I could do it. And then I worked six days a week – nine till nine – to pay it off. Find a way to take a night course, do weekend or evening work; there is night school, and there are further education courses. You can shadow someone. You can volunteer. I can't give individual advice if you've got dependents and bills to pay, but for everyone there will always be small baby steps that you can take.

2. Be uncomfortable. If you want to become the best that you can be, there will be times where you have to put yourself in uncomfortable positions. What is the worst thing that can happen? There's absolutely nothing that can go wrong that you can't come back from. And people have no place in criticising you if you're trying.

3. Keep learning. I've been intimidated by more knowledgeable entrepreneurs and I've been inspired by what companies do and the stories that you hear on social media. Stay open-minded and remember that what you see is only the tip of the iceberg; there is so much more that you don't know and can learn.

4. Build a support network. They can be clients or people you meet at networking events. I was always frightened of not feeling good enough to be in a social circle of entrepreneurial people. However, I went in with a mindset of what could I learn from these people? Not just in the beauty industry, but in any industry.

5. Understand people. Do your research. Read a couple of books on leadership skills, and learn how to best support different personalities, and the wants and needs of people.

THE
CONFIDENT *Beauty* THERAPIST
PROGRAMME

be.au.ty

/əm'pou(ə)r/ verb

be emotionally authentic and completely unique to you, treating others with the same kindness and respect.

@CONFIDENTBEAUTY

Definition of real beauty is to Be Emotionally Authentic Unique To You.

THE
CONFIDENT *Beauty* THERAPIST
PROGRAMME

Your can plant your seed but its the joinery that gives you the growth and
results. Nourish your business all the time.

"

Little by little,
one travels far.

J. R. R. Tolkien

*Its the leader we climb that gives you the big results so enjoy the little wins on
your way.*

Pure Perfection est 2015☐Barrowford, Pendle Lancashire. Recognition to Laura

4. FINDING YOUR SUPERPOWER

I n my first year of doing my Certificate in Education, it became clear that I wasn't a typical thinker. I had been handing in my assignments and mixing up the Bs and Ds. My sentences didn't make sense and every time I referenced a source, there was always a piece of the puzzle that was missing. I was writing 1000-word essays where my thinking and reasoning was just . . . different. I'd always had a feeling that reading and writing were weaknesses of mine; I just needed somebody to call me out on it. My tutor noticed that something was up, and suggested I get tested for dyslexia. When they confirmed that I was dyslexic, I felt so ashamed. I had wanted to prove to myself so much —that I was intelligent and worthy of my position. When I was diagnosed, I felt like a failure.

Years ago, when I was at school, dyslexia was not something that was ever discussed; it wasn't as openly accepted as it is today. So, I thought, 'Oh my God, if everybody knows that I have dyslexia, they'll treat me differently.' *They'll bully me.* It was a knock to my confidence, so I kept it quiet and didn't tell anybody. Again, that feeling of 'I'm not good enough' kicked in and I kept asking myself, 'Why am I so different?' I think my tutor could see the sheer panic on my face. She could see those questions going around in my head: 'Am I not good enough?' 'What do I do now?' 'How am I even going to finish this course?' So she reached out and gave me extra tuition and did it with such decorum and respect that I was never made to feel bad for the extra help. Of course it was her job to do that, but in my naivety her attention made me feel special. I was like, 'Oh wow, this woman is investing her time in me. She's going to help me because I haven't got a clue.' It made me feel like I could do it. She showed me how to process information and how to look at different resources, how to do things in smaller chunks, and how to find a way to relate to the information. I learned a lot from her and I am so grateful that this woman even gave up her time for me. Just because information for me goes in one ear and comes out the other doesn't mean that there's something wrong with me, it's just that my brain processes things differently. And it's the same for you. If you struggle with reading and writing, or you struggle to hold onto information, it doesn't mean that there's something wrong with you. It just means you think differently. It's your superpower – you just have to figure out how to use it.

But even with her help, there were times where I doubted myself. How could I even teach somebody a skill when I have dyslexia? Even after I graduated, and for a long time afterwards, I carried a lot of shame around it. I was such an independent person – I refused to be labelled and I never wanted to be seen as different. I never allowed my self to explore dyslexia any further – not until I met my business coach, and I'll talk more about her in the next chapter.

At that point, I was so focused on my business, that my self-development stopped at that point. I didn't tell anyone because I didn't want to be seen as a complainer or a victim.

So, for me, it was a case of having to find a different way to succeed. Instead of working with my weaknesses, which is what I do today, I ignored it and pushed it away. But dyslexia is part of who I am. At that time, I didn't realise how important it was to accept all parts of yourself. Burying your head in the sand is not going to help you if you're facing a challenge, and it isn't something that you should ever do. But that's what I did. Over the next decade, I denied part of who I really was, and – I'll be honest – it was painful. I carried a mixture of shame, feelings of failure and childhood trauma into everything I did. I should have stopped to heal and accept myself, but I was afraid it would stop me achieving my goals in business (how wrong I was!). So, I just parked the disability there, and found different ways to move forward.

What My Weakness Taught Me

Everybody's got strengths and weaknesses. And when you identify yours, you should absolutely run with it, whether it's a strength or a weakness. When I was diagnosed, despite feeling like a failure, it also gave me a little bit more drive. I thought, 'So, if this is how my brain works, how can I make it work for me?' And this was something that I began to explore with my business coach later in my career. If you face an obstacle, what can you do to make it work *for* you instead of *against* you? It will be a really, really difficult process to go through because you are exploring your weaknesses not your strengths, but there will always be someone there to help you. Just ask for help: ask a friend, a colleague, a teacher, someone you admire. Yes, you may have a weakness, but that doesn't mean it should defeat you. If you start something, you should finish it. Use your weakness as a springboard to push you forward rather than hold you back. I wasn't good at reading or writing but I knew that I was really good at being hands-on and I understood the world by how things felt and how I experienced things. So, that how I was going to teach my apprentices.

One of the most important things that you can do is to explore your own self-awareness. Explore how you think, and how you process information. Take some free tests online. You'll find free dyslexia tests, free ADHD tests, free personality tests. I think that as human beings we're not taught any part of psychology in school and it's such a shame because it's so important to understand that there are other people in the world that think differently to you. And that's really normal, so go and explore why you feel like you feel and why you think like you think, and start getting some answers.

I had to find different ways of learning business without going down the traditional route. If I had, I would have failed; I really would have failed because I would have been measured against rules and requirements that weren't right for my situation. And I probably would have blamed myself for it. And I might have quit. Exploring different ways of learning – and knowing that I didn't have to do things the neurotypical way – freed me to find my own direction and made me feel better about my education. For me, learning on the job was the best way of understanding how it felt and what it looked like. At the end of the day, that was the best training exercise I could have ever asked for. In a strange way, my refusal to accept dyslexia has actually helped me, but that's my journey and I'm not saying that you should ignore part of yourself. My journey would have been a lot easier had I just allowed myself to accept who I was. In a way, what I saw as my weakness became my superpower. It pushed me to try harder and be better, and it sent me off in a direction that I might never had tried. If you feel you have a weakness, in anything, could it actually be your superpower?

Ignoring Failure

For a while, everything was working – until I wanted to take the business in the next direction. I wanted recognition. I felt that at that time, I had a really unique business model. I'd worked hard for it and I'd created success, and I wanted to be recognised for it. There's no shame in saying that we want recognition for our work. In a way, I also wanted people to see that the beauty industry should be recognised too – recognised as a real business. The people who run salons are *business*people who have just as many challenges and achievements as other business people in other sectors. Beauty deserves to be recognised as a valid sector within the economy.

However, my first application for the Business Awards was a big flop. Instead of just accepting the failure, I reached out to the Business Awards coordinator and asked for some feedback. The coordinator's feedback was very factual, and very honest, and gave some really good guidance on what it was that the judges were looking for. If I read that application now, I would be really embarrassed. There was no evidence and it was just loaded with nice fluffy words. It was not professional at all and it was very much as if a beauty therapist was spinning a story about business. I knew that my writing and reading skills were holding me back, but instead of quitting I worked closely with my business coach to make sure that I did better next time. It took me three years to win it, but I did it. I didn't want to be defeated.

Instead of letting dyslexia stop me, I found someone who could help me overcome the challenges. Always be open to feedback. Even if you don't like the answers, it just gives you clarity on what needs to be improved and it really does improve your skills. I think that if we all approach feedback like the positive experience it should be, the world would be a much nicer place. It's just how people deliver feedback that's not so good. That's where understanding different personality traits, and communication, really does help.

It's Never As Bad As You Think

In a way, you could say that my challenges when I was younger and my dyslexia gave me the fight and the drive to succeed. Up until that point, the Business Awards had never had a category for beauty, and had never recognised beauty and wellness as a 'real business.' By entering the awards and becoming part of that community, I began to change the way that people thought about beauty – and it changed the way I saw myself too.

However, soon after I began to win these awards, imposter syndrome starting appearing again. I never thought you could get over impostor syndrome but I've managed to actually get over the fear of not feeling good enough in new environments; this is because I take the approach of 'What's the worst that could happen?'

It's OK to want to go and find other types of people and communities that can help you get where you need to go, but you will need to step outside your comfort zones and there will be times where you feel like an impostor. But, if you push past that, you will meet some incredibly inspirational people and have some amazing experiences. There are people that I would never have spoken to five years ago; I'd be like, 'Oh my gosh, they're amazing at what they do,' but now it's not so scary. What's the worst thing that could happen? Once I went to an awards ceremony, and tripped up the stairs in front of *hundreds* of people. Embarrassing, yes. But is that the worst thing? I'm still here to tell the tale.

I remember once absolutely dreading going to a networking event. I felt like an imposter. I was 'just a beauty therapist.' I think there were about four women and everyone else there was male. I was so out of my comfort zone, it was absolutely unreal. I was put on this table with ten men and we all had to do a 30-second presentation of what you do and why you're here. I had no idea that we had do that and I felt physically sick. So, when it was my turn, I stood up in front of these intimidating, suited and booted men. I said, 'Hi, I'm Carla. I'm a beauty therapist, nice to meet you.' That was my entire 30-second presentation, and I could see all these men staring back at me, just with blank faces. I went bright red and I just had to play the 'blonde card' because they were all in stitches and all they talked about for the next half an hour was how to paint nails. It was awful, and I'd never do it again. However, once you've experienced something like that, everything else becomes so much easier in comparison. And if I can do that and not absolutely die, then what else can I do? I think getting comfortable with putting myself in uncomfortable positions has been another superpower that I've developed over the years. Because without putting myself in those awkward situations, writing terrible applications and being totally out of my depth at networking events, I never would have gotten to where I am today.

When I finally accepted my dyslexia, it was like a light bulb moment – as though a massive weight was taken off my shoulders. I'll be honest, it took a long time and I've only really accepted it in the last year. When you put yourself under that amount of stress for a long period of time, it has mental health consequences. It wears you down. So it's really, really important that if you do feel overwhelmed or ashamed or anxious or depressed that you find someone that can support you and that you look for answers. Asking for help is not a weakness; if anything, it's a massive strength. I think it's pretty much impossible to learn and retain every element of business as well as staying emotionally happy and mentally healthy. You can't do it alone.

Core Beauty Tips

1. Value and accept who you are as a person. And remember that you can change, if you want to. You can learn how to process information differently, learn new skills, and find new ways of being.

2. You don't know what you don't know. And at the time I didn't know that a lot of entrepreneurs don't go down the traditional route of learning – they find different ways. If you think about it, it's quite inspirational how some of these diverse thinkers actually do what they do, and that was a game changer for me.

3. Don't take your education for granted. I've met beauty therapists that have qualifications but have never been in a salon. I even have a friend that's got a law degree, and she doesn't do anything with it. I massively admire anybody that has skills, but if you've got these qualifications, but you aren't doing anything with it, find the courage and confidence to action them.

4. It's normal to feel out of your comfort zone. However, everyone feels like that. Don't use that feeling as an excuse to stop trying to do things that could help you. Try and join free communities online to support you.

5. Be aware of your strengths and weaknesses. Use them both to your advantage. If you have a strength, use it to help others; if you have a weakness, find ways to work around it – use it as a springboard or get someone to help you.

THE
CONFIDENT *Beauty* THERAPIST
PROGRAMME

Core values are so important, care about your work and you will never work for a living.

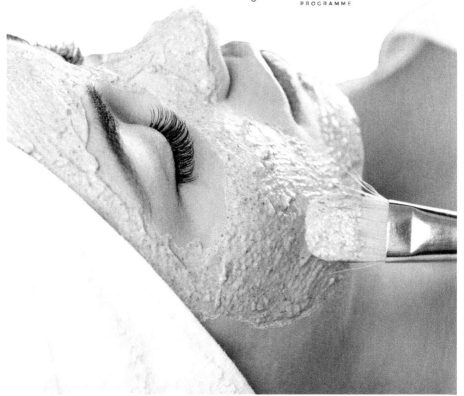

It's never just a facial, it's about the journey pf the mind and the results.

THE
CONFIDENT *Beauty* THERAPIST
PROGRAMME

Remember you are more than just a beauty therapist. It's about the service and the full client journey.

The great thing in the world is not so much where we stand, as in what direction we are moving.

Oliver Wendell Holmes

Create you own opportunities as you grow. Our choices matter in the direction you want to grow.

Thankyou for coming in today, we're so
happy to see you!
Now just relax and enjoy, you're in
good hands.

Create your salon environment so everyone feels special and valued every
time. Consistency is key.

5. ASKING FOR HELP

'I can't believe I'm paying someone to call me out,' I complained. There I was, the owner of three salons, a business woman and employer of 20 staff, and I was being put in my place.

'This is called accountability, Carla,' my business coach replied, straight to the point.

'Ugh, I really don't want to do this,' I grumbled, but I trusted her. So, I opened my laptop and got on with all the tasks I had been avoiding. And it's been like this for the past 10 years. One thing you have to know is that no matter how successful you become, you cannot do it on your own. When you start your beauty journey, you go to college, you learn all about the body, about risk assessments, health and safety, how to look after your clients, the full anatomy and physiology of the body – and after three years of hard work you have all the skills you need to perform exceptional beauty treatments. But how do you manage self doubt and imposter syndrome? Who will help you to choose between being self-employed or starting a business? Who do you talk to when you worry you aren't being a good employer, or that your team isn't performing the way you want? The beauty industry is a world that's extremely challenging; none of that is taught, so you need people around you who can help.

I got to a stage where I was managing three salons and 20 staff, and I had two small children at home. On the outside I might have looked like I had it together, but inside I was lost. I was doing everything I thought that I should be doing to be successful, but every day I got a little bit more lost. I didn't have the skills or understanding that I needed to get the result I wanted. I was overwhelmed and didn't know which way to turn. I got to a point where I was so fearful and out of my comfort zone that I was exhausted and constantly living in fear. I felt like I was doing everything blind. Hand on heart, if you keep running on that hamster wheel and doing the same thing over and over again, expecting a different result, as Einstein said, that is the definition of insanity. And that was me. But I get why people do it. There was so much more that I needed to learn but I was afraid of asking the stupid questions. Business is a very cut-throat environment, and I found it difficult to trust people and admit that I was struggling. I was an extremely independent person and I believed that success came from doing it on your own, so I didn't ask for any help.

My mum had a really good friend who was really high up in HR. She had a business degree and a psychology background, and had all this experience managing people. We'd met a few times at social events and every time we talked about business she would ask the kind of questions that made me think about the things that I wasn't doing. She was a business coach and could see that I was really struggling in business. I was hiding behind a big smile, but was suffering emotionally inside and she knew it. She reached out and said, 'If you ever need any help with business, this is what I do.' But I had a belief that people should lead by example. Walk the walk. So, I couldn't understand how someone who wasn't a beauty therapist could understand what I was going through. This mindset made it harder for me to find people within the beauty industry that I could trust with my problems, but I needed help and I trusted her, so I agreed – and it was the best decision I ever made. I feel like I actually got the jackpot when I met this women. She became my business coach and confidante, my right-hand wing-woman. Asking for help was like meeting my guardian angel.

Think Outside of the Beauty Box

People think that being a CEO of a company or a small business is just telling people what to do, and sitting behind a desk reaping the financial rewards, but that's so far from the truth, it's unbelievable. We wear so many different hats, and not all of them fit naturally. Some of them don't fit at all, and it's OK to find someone who can do it better than you to help you. When I started working with my business coach –who also became my life coach – she soon started working with me on the things that I needed to do to run a successful business. Having that outside perspective taught me so many things about myself and about the type of beauty therapist and business owner that I wanted to be.

Firstly, I realised that my brain works very fast – making decisions instinctively without thinking things through. And I'm a very emotional person too; it'a strength, but this can also be a weakness in business. I very much care about people's opinions and making everyone feel comfortable; it's something that I'm proud of and it's what I've built my business on. But sometimes you have to actually make decisions based on facts, and take time to think things through. That was an insight that could have only come from outside my world view. You cannot please everybody, no matter how much of a people-pleaser you might be. The bottom line in business does matter and you cannot make decisions that are always based on your emotions. If you can work from a place of facts, I think you get a lot more respect from the staff, and clients, because they understand the reasons behind it. And they know it's not emotional or personal.

This outside perspective has helped me to structure my company, and develop really crystal clear roles and responsibilities, systems and processes. I began thinking about my team as individuals and how I could help them in their careers. You can't assume that everybody thinks like you and has the same values and drivers as you. Every single person in the world is unique. Your culture, age, ethos, values – just everything. One size doesn't fit all and I had to work with my business coach to identify what it was that drove our team. Stopping to think about this outside perspective will allow you to see the roadblocks clearly and to make changes before you get stuck. If not everyone thinks like you, then you need to make sure that you're really clear on who you are as a company – or freelance beauty therapist – so that you can build the best business for you and attract the right clients for you. I quickly realised that I wasn't very clear, and my communication skills were really poor. I had to learn how to ask the open-ended questions so that I could find out what people really thought. You'll soon meet people who value work-life balance, some people value recognition and rewards, and some people will really value the team culture. When this happens, you'll have a lot of work to do on incorporating this into the way you work. When I did this, it massively opened my eyes to making sure that I accommodated everybody's needs.

I learned so much from working with a coach that asking the right questions in a coaching style has inspired how we do consultations with our clients. What we have in our heads is very different from what's in a client's head, so being able to identify what they want out of the service is really, really important and is a key element in your role as a beauty therapist. What does your client *really* want out of their treatment, because sometimes it's not about the treatment – it's about how the journey, or you, makes them feel. When a client comes in and says, 'I want my eyebrows doing,' you have to consider what kind of style works well with their face. Is their idea of a glamour brow the same as your idea of a glamour brow? Do they really want this service or do they just want to look like their friends? Why do they really want a glamour brow when a natural brow will make then look ten times better? We all leave school knowing maths, english and science, but we don't learn core skills like communication and human psychology and empathy. These are all essential skills that beauty therapists need in order to deliver effectively to give people the best experience.

Questions For You

When you start as a beauty therapist, you need to identify who you are as a business. What do you represent? Why are you doing it? What kind of clients do you want to serve? When I learned this, I was like, 'Oh my gosh, I've never even thought of these before.' One thing that I didn't understand about coaching was that they're not allowed to give you the answers. It's all about asking the right questions to help you find the answers on your own. So, here are some questions that she'd ask me, that might help you too:

- What is your unique selling point?
- What do you want to be valued for in the beauty industry?
- What do you think makes a great beauty therapist?
- What are your own core values?
- What does success look like to you?

Just take some time to think about these questions and find the answers. It is so important to be open-minded and to realise that you will always have gaps in your knowledge.

My Secret Ways to Learn

From a really young age, I learnt that if finances are a problem, you have to find another way. I never had the finances to fund business growth, so I pretty much had to go and find out the information, the hard way. Time was my most valuable asset, and I used it wisely – to learn. After all, Google is free. And I spent a lot of time googling how to do this, or how to do that. If you see something, or feel something, and you don't understand it, then be curious and go and explore what it means. Don't fear something just because you don't understand it. I have a real fear of words because there are so many fancy words out there. But using Google and pretending to be a 'dumb blonde' got me everywhere because it gave me permission to not have all the answers. I learnt so much by giving up my time, too – like doing free educational sessions in schools. When I first met my business coach, she knew that I came from an underprivileged background. I might have been running three salons, but that didn't mean I could afford a coach. So, I was really fortunate that she suggested that we did coaching in return for a year's worth of free beauty treatments. There is always a different way to solve a problem by exchanging skill sets with others.

Every single client that you meet will have skills and knowledge in an area that you don't. So, I would encourage you to just have an open conversation with them and learn from them. The clients will love it because they get to talk about themselves, and who doesn't love talking about themselves? They get a relaxing beauty treatment and you get to create a connection with someone who can teach you something new. I call my clients my diamonds because they have supported me in so many ways that they're unaware of. Even though they've come to me for a service, I've met so many people in diverse jobs and industries – people that have trusted me enough to share their industry insights. And actually when you do this, you'll find that all businesses are run the same. They just have different goals, different objectives, and different fields. Even running a school or a doctor's surgery is still a business.

Even if the corporate world is on a bigger scale, we all have to have certain policies and procedures; we all have to have targets and have to generate enough funds to be able to pay the overheads. Just by talking to your clients, and being a listener, you will hear how other people work and you'll find it reassuring. When I did this, I was like a sponge. This knowledge was free, and it was coming from a valuable source. Knowledge really is powerful, but you've got to understand that actions have to come with it as well. It's not enough to talk to people and learn, you have to action everything that you learn as well. What's the point of having all this insight and knowledge if you don't do anything with it?

Don't do it Alone

I've now had a coach for ten years. And you might think: why does Carla still need a coach? I still ask myself that question, too. And the truth is that my business is more successful with her than without her. I see her once a month, and we go through all the things that I need clarity on. I used to battle with her because she would say things that I didn't agree with, and that's fine. We never ever got into a conflict during our discussions. It was a healthy discussion and it was really fun to argue the different sides of things. There's no right or wrong answer. And there's no right or wrong view. For me, it's healthier to see my business – and my life – from different angles, and to make sure that I don't get tunnel vision. Having that person to help me tackle those problems means that I don't have to face things alone.

Being able to ask for help is probably one of the most courageous things that you can do. We can get stuck in the way we do things, but it can change everything to have someone experienced – and that you can trust – to say, 'What about this? Have you thought about that?' However, if you try and do everything yourself, well . . . you'll spend a very, very long time trying to figure everything out. If you can find someone that's walked the walk, and understands certain points, you'll make your life so much easier. Build honest business connections and collaborations with the right people, because there are so many people out there who can help you – and who *you* can help too. There's value in collaborating with people that have information and experience that you value. But do your research and find out what type of coach or mentor or confidante best suits your personality, and find your main drivers in terms of what it is that you're searching for.

There are now so many coaching programmes on the market that they can talk you through the step-by-step process and give you the tools and the resources that you need in order to develop. Obviously, if that's something that you don't want to explore, that's also OK. I'm not saying that everyone needs a coach or that outside perspective, but I think you'll go further and find more success if you're open to more outside help. I know that not everyone is fortunate to have a business coach or confidante, which is why I'm writing this book and why I built The Confident Beauty Therapist Programme. I want you to have everything that I wish I'd had when I started. My beauty journey was so much harder because of my limiting beliefs and refusal to admit that I needed help. If I had to relive my entire 20 years of business again, I really, really wish I would have had a coach or mentor at the start. It would have saved me a lot of time – and pain – on that emotional roller coaster. I wouldn't have had to figure things out backwards and the wrong way around, and failed so many times. I would have had someone to tell me not to torture myself when I failed, and that everything that I was about to experience – the highs and the lows – were all normal.

Core Beauty Tips

1. Do your research. There are so many business coaches out there. Find out what values they share, and obviously consider if you can afford it. If you can't find online courses, create your own network of people in business, or find an accountability partner that you trust.

2. Action your learnings. Listen to people and learn. They can give you free knowledge and insights on so many different things, and that is brilliant. But if you're not going to act on what they tell you, then you cannot expect things to change.

3. Your clients are your diamonds. They are probably the most important people. They're the ones that help you pay your bills and put food on the table. So, you've got to learn how to serve them at the highest level. I built relationships with a diverse range of clients regarding race, sexuality, gender identity and profession. I've worked with nurses, doctors, lawyers, police, entrepreneurs, business people and parents. When you build that relationship with them, that's when you can share advice, talk, and trade your expertise and advice with each other. That's your support network.

4. Don't compare yourself. Everybody has a different starting point in their business career. Some have financial backing, some people have more knowledge than others, some people have better connections. You'll never really know or understand what their story is and how they've started, so don't ever compare your business to somebody else's. Everybody's foundations are very, very different. And everybody's financial outgoings are very, very different. And people's goals are very different.

5. Keep improving your communication skills. It is a core skill, along with psychology and empathy, but it's not something that we're trained it. If you can keep getting better in these areas then you will become a beauty therapist that your clients cannot live without.

Self-Awareness
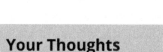
Categories

Your Thoughts
How do you explain and think about what happens to you? What's your self-talk like?

Your Emotions
How well do you understand your own emotions and moods? Do you observe and try to understand your emotions or do you react impulsively to them?

Your Behaviors
Are you aware of why you tend to act in certain situations the same way? What types of events trigger you?

CBT Therapy all starts with how you think about you and the world around you.

66

Move out of your comfort
zone. You can only grow if
you are willing to feel
awkward and uncomfortable
when you try something new.

Brian Tracy

When you become comfortable then look for your next move. There are
opportunities everywhere.

THE
CONFIDENT *Beauty* THERAPIST
PROGRAMME

Get educated, knowledge is power but it's the action that will get you the results.

Management team of 2015:Laura, Me, Tara, Adele. Create opportunities for others to grow with you, not for you.

6. WHEN IT ALL STOPS

When COVID hit, it was a transition that I don't think anyone was ready for. I became very, very aware that there were so many people suffering in the world, and there wasn't anything that I could do. Businesses were closing down, people were losing their jobs – losing their lives. Overwhelm kicked in and my brain went into overdrive. I had so much responsibility in terms of my team, my family and my business, but at the same time I had so little control. I had to close three salons down and find a way of keeping 30 people on my payroll. Myself and the team had spent nearly 20 years building up something special – I couldn't just make people redundant. But I had no idea how I was going to do this. I had to make sure that everyone's mental health was looked after, and keep their spirits up. I had to manage the finances, learn all the new laws and regulations – all while keeping a brave face. I had to study how to manage money and make sure that my outgoings were getting paid, and basically keep the businesses afloat and out of debt. It was probably one of the most traumatising experiences that I've ever had to go through. No one could see how tough it was behind the scenes. But it changed everything for me.

My Biggest Learning

Before COVID, I'd done a lot of work on what my strengths and weaknesses were. I was kind of on a roll, in terms of my self development and growth, and it was brilliant. I was working with a coach, I had a great team and a secure future. But I was still on that hamster wheel, working 12-hour days, and I was hyperfocused – almost obsessed – with success. But with COVID I had no option but to get off that wheel, and it was the first time that I really analysed what my success actually meant. And it was such a pivotal experience.

On paper, I had become a success. This dizzy blonde – that had come from an underprivileged background, who had dyslexia, who didn't know what the word 'strategy' meant, who'd had tables of men laugh at her and people underestimate her – had done everything she had set out to achieve. You'd think that I'd be on top of the world, but in reality . . . I was sad. I worked so many hours and was so focused on business growth, that I did stop to look after myself? I always put everyone's needs before my own. I never had family time. I very, very rarely saw my children. I had become that person that I never wanted to be. And I had lost track of what success was to me.

It doesn't matter how much money you've got in the bank; if you haven't got the time and the emotional happiness to enjoy the experiences that life brings you, what's the point? Is that really success? On paper I had everything I ever thought possible, but I wasn't living – I had no life. I went through a strange time of resenting my success and wealth, and I developed depression and anxiety. But because I'd never experienced those before, or really talked about it, I didn't know what was happening to me. When you are so out of control in terms of your own thoughts and emotions, it's like your body shuts down and your brain goes into fight or flight. The moment when everything stopped was the moment that I realised I was truly burnt out.

I never realised just how many people experience this, especially women – how much we have to juggle a career, and families and everything else, and do it on our own because it feels like we have more to prove and more things to jump over. Now that I've experienced it, I see it everywhere. I began to see that even though I prioritise external self-care – I moisturise, I get my brows done, I have massages and waxes, I work in the self-care industry – I never took time for self-care, *internally*. I never gave myself a pat on the back and told myself, 'Well done.' I had quite a lot of negative self-talk. And I never took time off. Never, never, ever took time off.

I was so hard on myself and I felt that I had to continue to learn to find ways to be better. I suppose it was that need for external validation – that drive to prove everyone wrong. But actually what I really needed to do was to use this time to stop and reflect. So, after I went through a couple of crying moments, I was like, 'Right. Come on, you can do this.' And, working with my coach, we used this time to look back over the last 20 years and see if we could create something positive out of something so difficult.

Look in the Mirror

When you stop and write down how many things you've achieved, it will be a pivotal moment for you. How many courses have you been on? How many clients have you helped? How many workshops or events have you hosted? Don't underestimate your knowledge: you're an expert in physiology, chemistry and biology. There's a lot more science involved in beauty than people think. What skills do you have? What knowledge do you have? You've got to be an artist, a therapist, a businessperson and a human being with a life too. It's not easy. One of my key drivers is to prove people wrong about the beauty industry. People think that this is the easy way to make a living and all we do is file nails – and I just want to scream at them. Being in this industry is so much harder than people think.

It was during COVID that the government finally announced that we had our own personalised sector: the self-care sector, and I couldn't have been prouder to be a beauty therapist. Our workers officially became recognised as people with unique qualifications, who had the right to be seen as professionals. So many men and women relied on our services, and when it was taken away during COVID, I think people's values and opinions on the industry changed. Some people will go to see you for their mental health more than the beauty treatment. If people struggle with body dysmorphia, or have mental health issues and anxiety, not being able to see that one person for such a length of time can be so debilitating. I remember that I had clients ringing me up in absolute floods of tears because nobody was there to wax their beard or control their acne. Our work is important and we do so much more than shape brows and file nails. So, take time to reflect on just how important the work you do is, how hard you've worked, and the impact you make. Your achievements matter.

When I stopped and reflected, I asked myself: What do I want to do now? Where do I want to take the salons? And what's important to me? I realised that by then my goals had changed and I was ready to give back my 20 years of experience, knowledge and expertise. And that was a massive moment for me. I really, really like going to work, and I like having a purpose. But I like being able to watch others succeed too. So even though COVID gave me zero finances for two years, and also very little profit, it gave me the time and space to think about other ways to achieve my goals, and, more importantly, realise my purpose. I discovered that I had the knowledge and a new mindset structure to educate others. And thats when the Confident Beauty Therapist training programme was born. Here was something that I could focus my time on, because this is where my purpose was. The business pivoted and we began focusing on something that could support therapists of the future. Even in the most difficult times, when we could have cried and buried our heads, we built something positive.

What is Real Success?

Coming from an underprivileged background, success – to me – was money. That was the goal – to never struggle for money, and if I wanted something I would have the opportunity to buy it. So, for my entire journey, the goal was to have financial wealth and for 20 years I worked for it. When COVID hit, I realised for the first time that on paper, I was a millionaire – and I felt frightened and ashamed. I had the belief that millionaires were greedy and that people who want money have poor values. I can't believe how ashamed I felt for wanting to work for money. So, I went and took a money mindset programme to figure it out.

Remember, like I said before, if something makes you uncomfortable, go and explore it and understand it, and see what it teaches you. On this course, we unpicked all the things that I was taught as a child and found that all my beliefs about money came from other people. They weren't my values; I had the choice to create my own values about money. You have the choice to create your own values and it's really important that you make your own story. We all value other people's opinions and we always want to please certain people in our lives. However, they are living their own stories, and it's not your job to live their story. We're so easily influenced by the things that people say or see, and if we're not careful we can very easily get crossed wires, misperceptions and misunderstanding.

It's really important to go and look for the evidence before you make decisions. Think carefully about what you choose to value and what is important to you – not what is important to anyone else. If someone important to you has a value that you really like, then take that value with you. But if they hold values that you disagree with, then question and explore that. My mindset and knowledge is very different to what my friends, work colleagues or husband have. And that's OK. There's so much knowledge out there and some people choose to be more self-aware than others. And some people are just really happy in their bubble, not knowing what they don't know. And that's OK, too.

As we grow, our goals can change as we change. And I realised that I had reached a stage in my life where time was of much more value to me than money. And I had never valued time like that before. So, for me, my definitions of success and wealth changed. It was about self-care – internally as well as externally. It's about looking after our minds, and looking for new and different ways to help people. This book came from that pivotal time in my life, and that's why, for me, it was the worst but also the happiest time of my life. If you experience a hardship – a challenge that you think you'll never come out of – just remember this: there will always be a way out of it and a way to create something positive from it.

Core Beauty Tips

1. Take real time for internal self-care. It might be a bath, meditation or a walk. When things get overwhelming find a way that works to help you calm your internal nervous system.

2. It's OK to feel overwhelmed. It's OK to be fearful. What I've learned is that if you're always worried about the future, you're anxious. If you're always living in the past, it's depression. But being present is the best place to be. It's all that you can do now and it's the only thing that you have control over. So what can you do today?

3. Fill your cup first. Trying to pour from an empty cup is just impossible. So fill your cup first. Stay healthy and look after yourself internally so that you can drive your business forward – whether that's for your team or for your future.

4. Celebrate the small wins. If you want to wait for the big win, you could be waiting years and years, and, before you know it, 20 years could have gone. For me, a small win is still getting those reviews from a client, and knowing how much you've made a difference to someone's day. Stay connected to your core values – that's the biggest win, I think.

5. It's so important that you look after your mind. Stop giving yourself the negative self-talk. Look at the good things that you do and don't focus on the bad. It's all about your thoughts, your feelings and your behaviours. So, if you've got a negative thought, you need to find out why you feel like this and explore the behaviour, because our behaviour shapes the direction we will go.

THE
CONFIDENT *Beauty* THERAPIST
PROGRAMME

Something that is created by the worst times can pivot you into the best.

It is not the mountain we conquer but ourselves.

Edmund Hillary

Become so self aware and become the best version of yourself.

Celebrating business awards (winner of customer friendly category) Life Coach Debs Connell. Photo credits to Liz Henson.

Celebrating our ten years anniversary with the fabulous Pure Perfection Team, clients, family and friends.

7. BALANCING THE FUTURE

I read something recently that asked, 'Can women really have it all?' I think that's the wrong question to be asking because it's so unique and personal to each situation. I've learned that yes, you can have it all – but it depends on what 'have it all' is. And it depends on what 'having it all' means at different stages in your life. What is it that you want when you're starting out? When you're having a family? When you're in retirement? When I was younger, I thought that having it all meant being rich with a successful business, and understanding *everything* about it. But having it all doesn't always mean being financially rich and knowing all the answers. To some people, it could mean having more time wealth, health wealth or just more freedom to make your own choices.

After COVID and that time of reflection, I quickly realised that I had to change my goals and my idea of success if I wanted to be happy. Today, I think that 'having it all' means having balance. And, after COVID, it was the first time that I realised that I'd never had any before. When I started out as a beauty therapist, I was on a mission. The only way that I knew how to succeed was to do it all by myself. My thoughts were solely focused on being successful, knowing it all, having it all and doing it all. When I got married, we decided that my husband would give up his career to look after our children, so

I could invest in mine. It was an incredibly important decision that we agreed on together, but it came with its consequences; I suffered so much with mum guilt, and I missed out on precious time with them. My mental health and my emotional health was affected and I wasted a lot of time worrying, making mistakes and just struggling. Let's be clear, I don't regret any of those choices – it's brought me a lot of success and it's why I'm in the position I'm in today, but I know now that I could have done it differently.

Pure Perfection

The salons that I run are called Pure Perfection, and I never really understood why I called them that. I just knew I wanted to create excellence and perfection for my clients with Pure intentions. And I did. But perfection means different things to different people. And if you think about it, perfection doesn't really exist. Seeing so many women and men suffer with low self-esteem and body image because they believe they have to be perfect makes me want to fight to find better ways to engage with our beauty ideals. We need to address and understand mental health and its relationship to beauty and wellness, but if we don't, our industry is going to split into different directions. I don't want my clients to feel that they all *have* to have a certain look or style to be accepted and we educate our staff members to look for signs of anxious clients, depressed clients, clients with eating disorders, and clients with neurodiversity. And that's something that I'm passionate about.

I want to be really clear that I understand that the aesthetic industry has very clear goals and objectives and wants to help people fix the external problems that they're not happy with. And I completely understand why they're doing that. But I do think we need to introduce a little bit of psychology and empathy to our work, and find out *why* people are coming to us for beauty treatments. In our salons, we believe it's about enhancing what you've got and just fine-tuning and grooming yourself. The beauty industry has so many different avenues, and we only see what marketeers let us see, so go and explore what it is that you want out of the beauty industry. Go and explore the things that you don't always see, or the parts of the industry that aren't so glam. Find that balance in your own understanding of beauty.

Understanding your own values and where you sit in the market is really important because then you'll have a clearer message and your clients will know what to expect from you. Identify what route you want to go down, but don't forget to explore the rules, procedures, the pros and cons, the legalities, and the qualifications that you'll need in order to ensure that you're a fully educated and informed therapist. Really do your homework. Balance doesn't come easily, but it's worth working for.

How to Find Balance

If you find yourself feeling out of balance, which we all do from time to time, there's nothing wrong with stepping back, simplifying things and changing the way you work. Stepping back will help you to see the wood for the trees. I knew things had gotten out of balance when I was tired constantly, had memory loss and was suffering with anxiety. I didn't eat very well, I used alcohol to soothe me, and I spent money on things that were just not worth it. But, I didn't listen to the signs and it took a global pandemic to force me to change, but you don't have to do that! If you start seeing the signs then listen and take a step back.

Firstly, write down your goals and values. Putting it down on paper, just gives you a little bit of clarity on which direction you want to go in, because we can very easily get distracted and influenced by all the shiny stuff, all the different opinions, and different people. And that's all OK, it happens. However, keeping your own mind clear on your own goals is the main thing. It's all about understanding what's important to you. Is it children? Is it family? Is it nice things? Is it travel? When you do actually write it down, it's like, 'Oh wow, I didn't realise that was important to me.' And there are no wrong answers. Whether it's *I just want to be an award-winning nails tech,* or *I want to run my own salon,* or *I want to be a makeup artist that travels around the world,* or *I want multiple businesses,* or *I want to bring out a skincare brand.* There are so many different options in in the beauty sector and there is enough room for everybody. So, get clear on your goals and values.

Once you know them, be really strict and stick to them. It's all about discipline, boundaries and respect. Because of what I call my divergent mindset, there was chaos in my head and I had to develop a schedule planner that worked for me. I needed something to help me manage my boundaries, and help me change my mindset in different situations so that I could be at my best. So, when I'm in my office, my mind is on work. When I'm in my home, it's family time. When I'm in the salon with clients, I'm a beauty therapist. When I'm networking, I'm selling being an owner and manager. I created boundaries and I'm really disciplined with them. I know that Monday is my admin and accounts day, and then once I've done that I have 'Me' time. I have my PT session on a Tuesday morning, and Tuesday afternoon I have stuff that I need to do for the house. Wednesday is my business day with my coach. On Thursdays and Saturdays, I work with clients. And on Friday I have another admin day. I have clear structures, and I do not overlap or change them. If I do, my wires get crossed and things start getting misunderstood. I tried all sorts of different methods and structures until I found one that worked. Find what works for you, and keep trying until you find something that sticks.

Find the mentors and educators that can help you reach that goal, too. Remember that you don't have to do it all and know it all yourself. Finding someone who can help you will give you a more balanced approach. All the information is free on the internet, you just have to look. Don't be frightened of getting in touch with people who can help you, either. There are a lot of free support networks out there. And yes, there is a cost attached but it depends on what you value. Do you want to buy a pair of Louis Vuitonn shoes, or a handbag? Or do you want to invest in your education to get to different stages of your career? Think about the bigger picture.

Respect everybody's opinions and values, and learn from those that have actually walked the walk and not just talked the talk. I do have a dyslexic mindset and know how important words are, and I am quite gullible. So, I did do a lot of fact finding and making sure that I understood the true meanings behind what people are saying. Don't just listen to what other people are saying but look at what they're doing, too. Actions speak louder than words, and if people aren't doing what they are saying, that's a problem. This is where trust and authenticity comes into play, too. I know I probably would have felt so much more happy putting myself in situations being my vulnerable, dizzy, blonde self, than I would have been pretending to be something I'm not. People accept you better when you're not hiding who you are. And if you do open up your vulnerabilities to people that have walked the walk, it's such a respectful and educational experience.

One Last Lesson

Everything that I'm telling you in this chapter and in this book, I had to learn over the last twenty years. Some of it I had to learn with my coach, some of it I read in books, and some of it I just realised for myself. If anyone had told me how much work actually went into running my business, I wouldn't have believed them. I was so drawn to the external bling and external validation that I didn't imagine there could be so much more to doing this job. It's the Iceberg Theory, isn't it? All people see is the success (the tip of the iceberg) but people never see all the mistakes, stress and hard work that goes on underneath. (If you want to know more about the Iceberg Theory, I encourage you to google it.) It's why I've written this book and created the CBT programme, because there's so much more to being a confident and successful beauty therapist than people realise.

Part of what goes on underneath is understanding that everybody starts their journey from a different place. Think of it like being dealt a card in a card game. Someone might start at a two, some might start at a king, and some might start at a nine. Everybody starts at different points, and it's not just in terms of starting off wealthy or not, it's also about knowledge, manners, values, education, culture and ethnicity. There are so many diverse elements that create one person, and that means everyone's future journey will be just as diverse. When you understand that, know that if you've been dealt a lower card than somebody else, that's OK. It's not a reason to quit or proof that you're not good enough. It just means that you have to find the knowledge to get onto the next level. And if you're at higher level, maybe there are pieces of knowledge that you're missing in order to understand diverse backgrounds.

You've just read this book and now you know that I was dealt a lower card. But, all that people see is the the tip of the iceberg – my salons and awards, and my team. People don't see everything that I've just told you in this book. They don't see that it took me twenty years, and that I went from apprentice to nail specialist to brow specialist to facial specialist to senior therapist, and then onto a management position. I had to learn all about accounting, employment law and marketing strategies. I had to learn about communication skills, how to identify strengths and weaknesses, and how to build a successful team. I had to learn how to be a leader, a marketeer, an area manager, a lecturer, and a trainer. Now, I'm becoming a mentor and a coach. But no one sees all of that when they look at me; they only see the end result.

For anyone starting in this industry, I want you to focus on what's personal and important to you, and not what you *think* everyone else is doing or what you think success *should* look like. I think if you forget everything you've just read, I want you to remember that. The Iceberg Theory. Just because everyone knows how to look beautiful and successful, it doesn't mean that they are. If everybody understood the Iceberg Theory, and remembered it, it would make people so much more caring, understanding and compassionate. It's a game changer.

Core Beauty Tips

1. Don't be so hard on yourself. If you're an apprentice, you're not going to be running a salon in six months. And if you're a nail technician, you're not going to be winning awards within a year. It's about being realistic and remembering the context that you're in. Learn everything as well as you can, and then move on to the next goal. If you you choose to stay there, or move in a different direction, that is fine. But don't expect growth if you're not prepared to put in the time in order to understand the steps.

2. Identify your purpose and passion. You will find your profit. If you put your profit first, you will never find fulfilment. So make your purpose clear and set your goals, lists and daily habits.

3. Have a good work ethic. People have to go to work to earn money. And I chose to work 12 hours a day, seven days a week, but that doesn't mean you should too. it's about choice and about understanding your own path, your own work ethic and sticking to your own business goals. The money will eventually come through success if you stick to your purpose and your why, and invest in growth opportunities and self-development.

4. Be yourself. Everybody looks different. Everybody acts different. Everyone has a different starting point and end point. You don't have to grow a huge career if you don't want to. You don't have to be a beauty therapist or a freelancer if you don't want to. Only you get to decide.

5. Find the balance. And balance means different things to different people. Take a step back to understand yours, and when you find it work on protecting and maintaining those boundaries so that you keep the balance in your life.

THE
CONFIDENT *Beauty* THERAPIST
PROGRAMME

Modern manners - respect works both ways and it's free. Write a list of whom you want to learn from.

I am where I am
because I believe in
all possibilities.

Whoopi Goldberg

Anything is possible, you always have choice, are you a cup half full or a cup half empty?

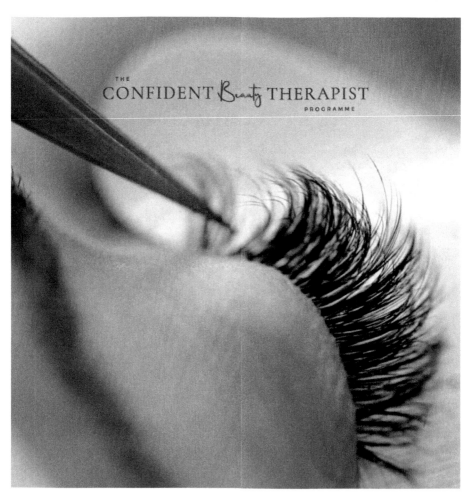

It's never just a lash service, it's about creating confidence and enhancing your own natural beauty.

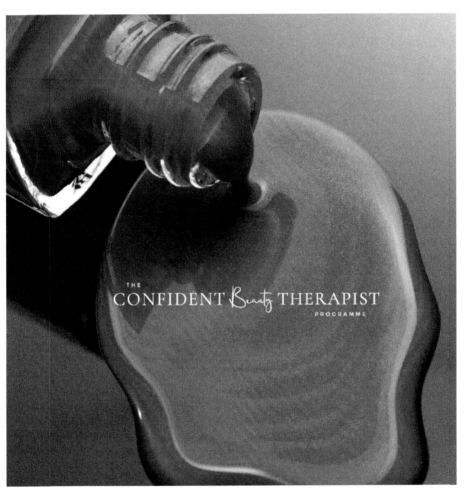

THE
CONFIDENT *Beauty* THERAPIST
PROGRAMME

Everything happens for a reason, are you asking the universe the
right questions? The secret lies with you.

CONCLUSION

At the time that I started my career, there was very little knowledge and education in the beauty business industry outside of the essential beauty training. There was no awareness of business, or self-development or *internal* beauty training. We weren't seen as a business industry in its own right, so we were all working blind, trying to build careers despite our lack of knowledge. But I think it's really important to bring that awareness to what small businesses do in the beauty industry. There's so much more to this work than people realise, and I think the perception of the beauty industry is completely changing. We've had to up our game on legal roles and responsibilities, we've had to up our game on strategies, demonstrate profitability, and demonstrate career growth for longevity and support in the industry. COVID proved that we are an industry that people can't live without – not just for external beauty but for internal beauty too. The beauty industry is a powerful and essential part of the economy, so people need us to be the best we can be.

It's why I wanted to call this book A Beauty.Full Mind. Beauty really does come from within and it's all about how you think and feel about yourself and how you share that with others. There are not many places in the world that people can go to and have that one-on-one confidential conversation, whilst being pampered and made to feel special – to know that that everything's going to stay in that room and they're not going to get judged for it. It's a big job and our clients put a lot of trust in us to make them feel beautiful inside and out. I hope this book has helped you to get started on that journey and is encouraging you to think differently about being a beauty therapist. If you forget everything that I've taught you in this book, these are the most important Confident Beauty Therapist tips.

Confident Beauty Therapist Tip 1

To become a diamond, you have to put yourself under pressure. Nobody will do it for you. And that means doing new things and feeling uncomfortable. I think anything that's new and uncomfortable will be scary. And I think we're not taught as human beings how to step out of our comfort zones with confidence. The worst thing that can happen is that you fail and you try again, you fail and you try again. It's like riding a bike; I fell off that business bike so many times, it was too easy to give up. If you've tried something and it's really not for you, then that's absolutely fine. But I feel that it's important that you know that those uncomfortable feelings are normal. You're not doing anything wrong. I just wish somebody would have held my hand at the time and said, 'That's OK, I've got your back. Everybody feels like this when they're trying something new.'

Confident Beauty Therapist Tip 2

Knowledge is power, but the small thing that people forget is it needs to be actioned. You can read all the inspirational quotes on social media, you can learn everything and know how to do everything. You can read this book and do my programme, but none of that matters if you don't put it into action. Accountability is massive, and everybody wants to be an entrepreneur, but not everyone is prepared to put the work in or do the time. It's now on you to go and explore what it is that you want out of your career. I can't do that for you.

Confident Beauty Therapist Tip 3

Find your own path. And remember, it's your journey. Find what's important to you and don't let other people's opinions of you affect you. If something's not working, go and find change. Turn negative feedback into positive action. Turn fear into excitement. It's OK to find different social circles and different friendship groups if you've outgrown the ones you used to have. This is your journey and nobody else's. Design it the way you want it to be.

Confident Beauty Therapist Tip 4

You don't have to do it all by yourself. Everyone's mind works very differently. Some people are emotional. Some people are logical. Accepting your weaknesses and strengths, and knowing when to ask for help, is a really powerful quality. Once you accept that nothing is ever certain, and that there will always be people to help you, you will find the whole journey a lot easier.

Confident Beauty Therapist Tip 5

Be your authentic self. I used to be really ashamed of my background and my upbringing. And I've only dealt with the shame over the last three years of my life. But I'm not embarrassed to share it anymore and I welcome any questions about it. I was born into a culture and environment that was tough, and I chose to make my culture and my environment better for me. And there's nothing wrong with that. Don't be ashamed of wanting to build wealth or create more time in your life. Don't be ashamed of your past; you cannot compare your story to anybody else's. And sometimes it's OK to feel that shame if you're going into different environments, but don't let it stop you. It's OK not to have all the answers, or all the skills. But it's all out there. We just have to go and find it.

Building a Beautiful Mind

I wanted to call this book A Beauty.Full Mind because we can all make judgements on somebody's success, but there is so much more to people's success than you know. You don't know what you don't know, and it's only through education and not comparing ourselves to others that we can create beauty – in ourselves and for others.

It's taken me 20 years to build up the confidence to share my knowledge with others and built the CBT programme. The inspiration for the name CBT actually came from Cognitive Behavioural Therapy, which I've been having for years. But it's also a Core Beauty Training. Core Business Training and Conscious Beauty Training. This is my purpose. I've put everything in one place so you can dig in and learn at your own pace in your own time. It's not a race, enjoy the journey ahead, and explore all the opportunities that cross your path.

The Next Steps On Your Journey

Thank you for reading my story. If you would like to learn more about the CBT programme, or to get in touch, you can do so here:

Website: www.confidentbeautytherapist.co.uk
Facebook: the confident beauty
Instagram: the confident beauty
Email: confidentbeautytherapist@gmail.com

Recommended Resources

Rich Dad Poor Dad - Robert T. Kiyosaki
Ego is the Enemy - Ryan holiday
The Secret - Rhonda Byrne
7 Habits of Effective People - Stephen R. Covery
Surrounded by Idiots – Thomas Erikson
The 4 Hour Work Week - Tim Ferriss
The Oz Principles – Roger Connors, Tom Smith and Craig Hickman
Employee Engagement - Kevin Kruse
Debs Connell - Wellbeing coach
Salon Boss mindset mastery- Jessica Crane
Julie Barrow Power Fit
TA Today Ian Stewart/ Vann Joines
How to Write a Book - Desmond Callaghan

15 Secrets to Successful Time Management - Kevin

Get Rich Lucky Bitch - Denise Duffield-Thomas

Ever Coach Mind Valley

Faster Than Normal - Peter Shankman

Diary of a CEO - Steven Bartlett

Reflections - Holly Willoughby

Meant for More - Mia Hewett

Playing Big - Tara Mohr

The ADHA in Adults Fix - Lawrence Conley

The Power of Habit - Charles Duhigg

Relentless - Tim S. Grover

Mind Management - Prof Steve Peters

The Chimp Paradox - Prof Steve Peters

The secret of getting ahead is getting started. The secret of getting started is breaking your complex overwhelming tasks into small manageable tasks, and then starting on the first one.

Mark Twain

Find passion and purpose in your beauty career with a positive mind of great attitudes of gratitude.

It starts with an idea, you are the only one that can make it grow. Be accountable for your own actions.

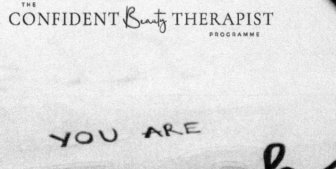

Remember your worth and run with feedback, it's priceless when you see this as a positive. Master your own mind.

Carla Chatburn

DIRECTOR

Hi, 39 years aliveThank you so much for taking the time to read my story, are you ready to start yours?

ATTITUDE OF GRATITUDE

I'm so grateful for all the help and support I've received from family, friends, my team and clients on my journey. It's been a tough road at times, but your love and loyalty have kept me going. Thank you from the bottom of my heart. You are truly amazing.

I would like to take a moment to acknowledge some personal people who have helped me more than you will ever know along the way. First, I would like to thank my mum (Julie) and Stepdad (Gary) for their support and love. I would also like to thank my friends and family, who have always been there for me and who have always inspired me. I am grateful for their continued support and loyalty. My amazing husband (Marcus), who is my rock and takes beautiful care of our two precious sons (William & Thomas).

My life/business coach Debs Connell who taught me so much. I am very grateful for her knowledge and wisdom. Shout out to all my business collabotors - Julie Barrow for keeping me focused and fit, Sean Mitchell for all our technical support, Jessica Craine (business coach), my former employer (Sarah), all our product suppliers, Trish for all your training. A huge thank you to all our clients and to the ones who we have not met yet, your support and loyalty have given me and my team so much more than just a service - you've inspired knowledge and given us the opportunity to build professional relationships and to serve you to highest level of customer care and personal development. Finally, I would like to thank all the team (past, present and future) who have helped me throughout my Beauty Business journey in creating three multi-award-winning salons (Pure Perfection) while supporting others education along the way.

Be grateful for what you have, even if it's not perfect

Often, we find ourselves focused on what we don't have, rather than being grateful for what we do have. It's important to remember that even if our lives are not perfect, there are still many things to be grateful for. Maybe we have a roof over our heads and food on the table. Or maybe we have great friends and family who support us. Whatever the case may be, taking the time to appreciate what we have can make a big difference in our overall happiness. So next time you find yourself feeling down about your life, take a moment to think about all the things you're grateful for. It might just brighten your day.

Photo dedicated to my lovely mum Julie, who did what she could with what she had.
So grateful and blessed.

Printed in Great Britain
by Amazon